40 Days to
Reclaiming
Your
Soul

DESTINY IMAGE BOOKS BY DR. CINDY TRIMM

Reclaim Your Soul

The 40 Day Soul Fast

40 Days to Discovering the Real You

40 Day Soul Fast Curriculum

CINDY TRIMM

40 Days to Reclaiming *Your* *Soul*

A COMPANION TO

Reclaim Your Soul

DESTINY IMAGE® PUBLISHERS, INC.

P.O. Box 310, Shippensburg, PA 17257-0310

"Promoting Inspired Lives."

This book and all other Destiny Image, Revival Press, MercyPlace, Fresh Bread, Destiny Image Fiction, and Treasure House books are available at Christian bookstores and distributors worldwide.

For a U.S. bookstore nearest you, call 1-800-722-6774.

For more information on foreign distributors, call 717-532-3040.

Reach us on the Internet: www.destinyimage.com.

ISBN 13 TP: 978-0-7684-0469-2

ISBN 13 Ebook: 978-0-7684-0470-8

For Worldwide Distribution, Printed in the U.S.A.

1 2 3 4 5 6 7 8 / 18 17 16 15 14

CONTENTS

	Introduction	7
Day One	Words.	11
Day Two	Objects	15
Day Three	Actions.	19
Day Four	Attributes	23
Day Five	Alliances	27
Day Six	Thoughts.	31
Day Seven	Mindsets	35
Day Eight	Attitudes	39
Day Nine	Beliefs	43
Day Ten	Paradigms.	47
Day Eleven	We versus Me	51
Day Twelve	Just versus Unjust	55
Day Thirteen	Interdependence versus Independence	59

Day Fourteen	"Contending For" versus "Competing With"	63
Day Fifteen	Win-Win versus Win-Lose	67
Day Sixteen	The Dynamics of Dysfunction	71
Day Seventeen	The De-Motivator of Shame	75
Day Eighteen	When Helping You Is Hurting Me	79
Day Nineteen	Spiritual Dimensions of Relationships	83
Day Twenty	Keep Watch!	87
Day Twenty-One	Pursue Destiny-Defining Moments	91
Day Twenty-Two	Pursue a Renewed Mind	95
Day Twenty-Three	Pursue Joy	99
Day Twenty-Four	Pursue Purpose	103
Day Twenty-Five	Pursue God's Presence	107
Day Twenty-Six	Value Boundaries	111
Day Twenty-Seven	Heed the Warning Signs	115
Day Twenty-Eight	Live Ethically	119
Day Twenty-Nine	Clearly Set Your Limits	123
Day Thirty	Respect Others' Boundaries	127
Day Thirty-One	Keep a Positive Expectation	131
Day Thirty-Two	See Past Barriers	135
Day Thirty-Three	Follow God's Lead	139
Day Thirty-Four	Lean In	143
Day Thirty-Five	Step Out	147
Day Thirty-Six	Listen	151
Day Thirty-Seven	Forgive	155
Day Thirty-Eight	Abide	159
Day Thirty-Nine	Bind	163
Day Forty	Pray	167

INTRODUCTION

This devotional is designed to be your daily companion on this 40-day journey to reclaiming your soul. The goal of the *Reclaim Your Soul* message is to empower you to break every type of soul tie that has kept you from experiencing the resilient life you have been created to live. It is about empowering you to cultivate more vibrant, life-enhancing relationships. With that in mind, I encourage you to walk this journey out with those you relate with most. Let this be a journey of healing for everyone closest to you. Use this daily devotional as a field guide for a small group study—or as a resource to strengthen your most intimate relationships.

There is nothing more wonderful than being set free— or more beautiful to watch than those you love finding the freedom they've longed for. Freedom is the fruit of empowerment. It was never intended to be a fleeting experience, but a *lifestyle!*

USING THE DEVOTIONAL WITH THE BOOK

Each day in this devotional matches the corresponding day found in Part Two of the *Reclaim Your Soul* book. The daily devotional is designed to help you put into practice the principles and disciplines taught in the book.

To take full advantage of this 40-day study, you should read each day's chapter in the book, and then follow up with the recap and activities found in the devotional. The questions, exercises, and activation prayers are designed to help you take what you've learned in the book and proactively apply it to your life. Gaining information only increases your bank of head knowledge *unless* you put hands and feet to it; then it becomes transformation—and that is where you are going with this journey.

I would encourage you to take 25-30 minutes out of your day and plan to use that to read your chapter and then work through the devotional. You can also break up your study by reading the chapter at one point in the day and then revisiting the devotional at another. It is important that you use this devotional with the book to get the most out of your experience.

Here is how the devotional is divided up:

DAILY DISCIPLINE

This simply reminds you of what the daily discipline is. It will be the same for both the book and for the devotional. These are key practices or habits essential to building a resilient life—they are the power tools that will enable you to break free and stay free in every area.

REFLECTION QUESTIONS

This is a great place to write down your thoughts and insights as you progress through the next 40 days. These questions are designed to get you thinking about and interacting with the material you read in both the book and devotional. Until you can really get your mind around where you stand in relation to each discipline, you won't be able to effectively incorporate them into your daily life. Remember, the devotional is yours. Make it personal. Complete transparency will allow the Holy Spirit to take your soul on a journey of freedom, healing, and empowerment.

ACTIVATION EXERCISES

Putting the disciplines into practice so that they become habits that turn into a lifestyle is the purpose of this journey. These exercises help you practically put into action what you've been learning and thinking about each day. They are not random. Rather, they are simple tools purposed to help you step out on what you are discovering and make progressive steps toward living out the daily discipline you've just studied.

EMPOWERMENT PRAYER

You will be able to seal every day with an empowerment prayer. I encourage you to pray the words that are written—out loud— and then use them to launch into your own personal time of conversation with God.

Be honest and be authentic. No one else is looking at this devotional. This is your opportunity to break every tie that has been holding you down and keeping you back from the resilient life you know God has destined you to live.

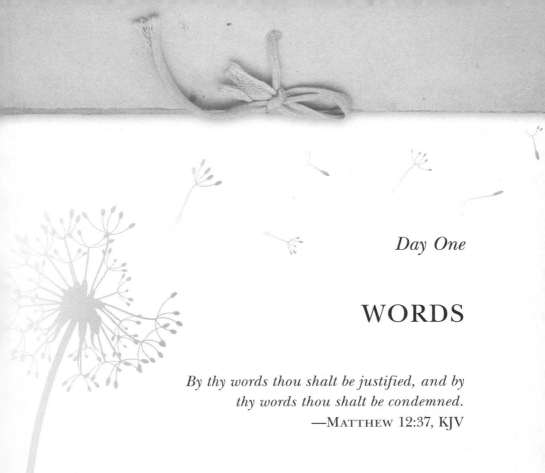

Day One

WORDS

*By thy words thou shalt be justified, and by
thy words thou shalt be condemned.*
—Matthew 12:37, KJV

Discipline #1:
USE YOUR WORDS WISELY

Our words are powerful. They have power, presence, and prophetic implications with no time or place limitations. In other words, many things that are happening in our lives can be traced back to the words we have spoken in the past—a kind of self-fulfilled prophecy. We create the future by the words we speak, which is a conduit of the thoughts we think. Whether internal private dialogues or audible expressions of our thoughts, feelings, and intentions articulated by sound, we can build or tear down our lives and the world in which we live. Like a plant wilts or thrives based on what kind of nutrients, water, and sunlight it receives, so do individuals, families, communities, and countries wilt or thrive based on words. *"Death and life are in the power of the tongue, and those who love it will eat its fruit"* (Prov. 18:21). The fruit of your words becomes the reality of your life. When you change your words, you change your reality.

REFLECTION QUESTIONS

Do you remember certain teachers you had in school who caused you to either wilt or thrive because of what they said?

_____

_____

_____

_____

_____

Have you ever said or thought something negative and then observed it come to pass?

_____

_____

_____

_____

_____

How often do you come into agreement with negative words being spoken about people or situations (whether it is in conversation or in the news) instead of listening to God's heart and perspective?

_____

_____

_____

_____

_____

_____

Who are some people who do an exceptional job of watching their words and speaking words of life?

_____

_____

_____

_____

_____

What is a step you could take toward guarding the words you speak and only releasing words of life?

_____

_____

_____

_____

_____

_____

ACTIVATION EXERCISES

Ask God to give you a mental picture of what happens in the spirit realm when you speak negative words. Then ask Him to give you a mental picture of what happens when you speak positive words.

Ask God to bring to your mind someone who needs encouragement—and then ask Him to help you craft it. Deliver that message however you wish.

Start a fund for the needy. For every negative thought or negative word spoken by you, your family, or close friends and associates, agree to give a dollar to that fund. At the end of every week or month, give it to someone less fortunate or to your favorite charity. Do this for a year.

EMPOWERMENT PRAYER

Say this out loud:

Dear Lord, give me grace to see the fruit of the words that leave my lips. Help me to be mindful of whether I am releasing words of life or death, and empower me by Your Holy Spirit to only release words of life.

I know that without You it would be impossible, so I choose to lean on You, listen, and yield to Your promptings. I choose to align myself with heaven's perspective and release words of life from Your heart so that Your will can be done on earth as it is in heaven.

Day Two

OBJECTS

Giving a gift can open doors.
—Proverbs 18:16, NLT

Discipline #2:
GIVE AND RECEIVE CONSCIENTIOUSLY

When we give or receive gifts with the intent to bribe, control, or manipulate, the outcome can be the formation of a soul tie. Some people may give gifts out of the sheer goodness of their heart, but others may give gifts in order to get something in return. Of course, we can do the same—even if not consciously. Giving gifts is not wrong; in fact it can be a reflection of God's loving heart when we give unexpected gifts because He gives so freely to us. Also, when David and Jonathan exchanged gifts as a token of their bond, it was a gesture blessed by God. However, we should always check any underlying motivation and whether the gift could potentially forge an unforeseen agreement or soul tie, and if that is something God wants us to do.

REFLECTION QUESTIONS

Have you ever given a gift with an underlying motive? If necessary, pray and ask God to sever the attachment.

_____

_____

_____

_____

_____

_____

Have you ever felt manipulated when someone gave you a gift—as if now you owe him or her something in return? Has anyone ever come back to make good on a "gift" by demanding that you do or provide something in return?

_____

_____

_____

_____

_____

_____

Do you feel that you have soul ties (good or bad) with people because of gift exchanges?

_____

_____

How does God give gifts to people?

How can the way you give gifts reflect God's heart?

ACTIVATION EXERCISES

Take a mental inventory of gifts you have received and ask the Lord if there are objects you own that were given to you out of an impure heart, and whether you should get rid of them. If the answer is "yes," find someone in need and give it to them anonymously if possible, as a blessing, expecting nothing in return. Also, ask God if there has been anything given to you by a former "significant other" that you should dispose of or give away. As you get rid of things, declare out loud that you are breaking ungodly soul ties with that person in Jesus' name.

EMPOWERMENT PRAYER

God, help me to freely give as I have freely received from You (Matt. 10:8). Forgive me for the times I have given gifts with impure motives (insert your own specific prayer). I choose to repent and, from this time onward, seek Your direction first.

Day Three

ACTIONS

Throw off your old sinful nature and your former way of life, which is corrupted by lust and deception. Instead, let the Spirit renew your thoughts and attitudes.
—Ephesians 4:22-23, NLT

Discipline #3:
PURSUE WHOLESOME ACTIVITIES

Engaging in unholy activities, whether they are done in reality, viewed on television, the Internet, a magazine, DVD, hologram, a phone, or in our mind, brings corruption to our souls. These activities can be engaged in alone or with other people. When other people are involved, ungodly soul ties attach with both the activity and the people and will result in unhealthy relationships and habits. The good news is that the power of sin and corruption upon our souls can be reversed through the blood of Jesus! It may feel like the allure of sin is stronger than holiness, but that can change in an instant (see Matt. 10:8; 2 Cor. 12:9).

REFLECTION QUESTIONS

Ask the Holy Spirit if there are any unholy activities you are currently engaging in that He wants you to stop.

_____

_____

_____

_____

_____

_____

What would the payoff be if you quit these activities?

_____

_____

_____

_____

_____

Are you ready to make a conscious decision to stop doing these activities?

_____

_____

_____

_____

Do you believe that the power of the cross is stronger than the pull toward ungodly behavior?

Are there people who engaged in sin with you from whom you need to disassociate yourself?

Activation Exercise

Think of someone who is trustworthy and godly (either your spouse or someone of the same gender) and designate a time when you can share your decision to stop engaging in any unwholesome activity. Do it now. Ask them to hold you accountable. Schedule a weekly time when you commit to connecting with that person for accountability purposes. There is power in numbers!

Empowerment Prayer

Say this out loud:

Thank You, Jesus, for dying on the cross to free me from sin and shame. I repent of engaging in (say what those activities are) *and I choose to loose those things and the consequences of those things from my soul. I receive Your forgiveness. Thank You, Holy Spirit, for the supernatural grace to change my desires and behavior from this day forward. Fill up my soul with Your light, love, presence, goodness, and holiness. Amen.*

ATTRIBUTES

Do you not know that your bodies are temples of the Holy Spirit, who is in you, whom you have received from God? You are not your own; you were bought at a price. Therefore honor God with your bodies.
—1 Corinthians 6:19-20, NIV

Discipline #4:
KEEP YOUR BODY HOLY AND SPIRITUALLY HEALTHY

You probably already know this, but there is a supernatural dimension that exists, consisting of good and evil—light and darkness. Satan masquerades as an angel of light, wooing people to darkness and evil through what appears to be acceptable, safe, exciting, and fun. God created each one of us with a spiritual vacuum and the innate desire to connect to God and His supernatural life source. So it is natural for us to desire the supernatural. We need to be careful what types of activities we participate in, however. If there is any activity that does not line up with the Word of God and His nature (see 1 Pet. 1:15-16), then we shouldn't participate in it. Satan can only counterfeit the real—which God created—so don't be unhappy about leaving certain activities behind; God has something so much better in store for you!

REFLECTION QUESTIONS

Are you compelled to read your horoscope, go to a fortune-teller, watch TV programs or movies with themes of magic or witchcraft, or participate in any supernatural activities that are not biblical?

_____

_____

_____

_____

_____

_____

Have you ever thought of these things being from the kingdom of darkness and polluting your soul?

_____

_____

_____

_____

_____

_____

_____

_____

_____

_____

Are you willing to leave these activities behind and see what God has in store for you instead?

_____

_____

_____

_____

_____

_____

_____

_____

_____

ACTIVATION EXERCISE

If there are any objects, books, games, DVDs, or other items in your possession that are associated with darkness or witchcraft, throw them away. Decide not to participate in dark activities any longer.

EMPOWERMENT PRAYER

Say out loud:

Jesus, I repent for participating in (list any witchcraft or dark activities you did or watched) *and I loose the effects of those things from my soul. I receive Your forgiveness. I choose to honor You from this day forward with my body, soul, and spirit. I don't want satan's counterfeit; I only want Your holy supernatural power. Holy Spirit, please teach me, help me to discern true light from darkness, and lead me to resources that can help me experience Your glorious supernatural power. Amen.*

Day Five

ALLIANCES

*If you have trapped yourself by your agreement and are
caught by what you said—follow my advice and save
yourself, for you have placed yourself at your friend's mercy.*
—Proverbs 6:2-3, NLT

Discipline #5:

BE MINDFUL OF YOUR ASSOCIATIONS

Different levels of relationships are based on varying ranges—
or circles—of trust. Our innermost circles, for example, might
include our heavenly Father, our parents, spouse, siblings, or
closest friends. And although we do certainly want to share
the love of Christ with everyone we meet and treat all people
with kindness no matter what their behaviors or beliefs are,
we should be mindful of who we let into our inner circles of
trust, because those are the people who will influence us the
most. Basically, trust is not an emotion, but a relational honor

bestowed upon someone who consistently demonstrates his or her trustworthiness. A circle of trust is built on mutually fulfilling and beneficial relationships undergirded by authenticity and the core values of love, care, honesty, integrity, authenticity, credibility, truthfulness, trustworthiness, and respect. There shouldn't be anyone in your inner circle with whom you don't have unquestionable confidence, assurance, and conviction concerning their character, values, and integrity.

This also pertains to organizations we affiliate ourselves with. In order to live life to the fullest, we must choose to allow our closest alliances to be kingdom-minded people and organizations—because we will ultimately resemble those with whom we assemble.

REFLECTION QUESTIONS

Are you mindful of whom you let into your circles of trust? List the specific individuals in each band beginning with those in your innermost circle, then move out to (2) close relations, (3) allies, (4) work/business relations, (5) neighbors, (6) acquaintances, (7) strangers, (8) enemies/threats.

_____

_____

_____

_____

_____

_____

_____

Have you ever felt uncomfortable because you accidentally let someone come closer than you should have?

_____

_____

_____

_____

_____

Are you afraid if you remove people from your life or walk away from organizations you've previously embraced (but could be an unhealthy influence) that there will be an empty space that could leave you lonely?

_____

_____

_____

_____

Do you trust God will meet you in that empty space?

_____

_____

_____

_____

_____

_____

Do you trust God will lead you to kingdom-minded people and organizations?

_____

_____

_____

_____

ACTIVATION EXERCISES

Ask the Holy Spirit to show you who you've let into your inner circle of trust that should be moved out. Ask Him what your relationship and interaction should look like.

Ask the Holy Spirit to reveal any organizations that you have affiliated yourself with that you should not be part of in this season. Ask Him for an exit strategy, record it, and implement it immediately.

EMPOWERMENT PRAYER

Dear Lord, I know that You created me to be in relationship with people and part of a healthy community. I want my closest friends and alliances to influence me to become the best person You created me to be, and in order to do that they should have a strong and healthy relationship with You. Please give me discernment to know who and what organizations I should align myself with and give my time to, so that I don't unwittingly slide away from You. Let's keep this discussion open. I give You permission to give me red flags when I am about to let an organization or person into a circle of trust. And I trust that You will meet all of my relational needs by giving me healthy, kingdom-minded affiliations. Of course You will always be in the center of my innermost circle of trust! I love You, Lord!

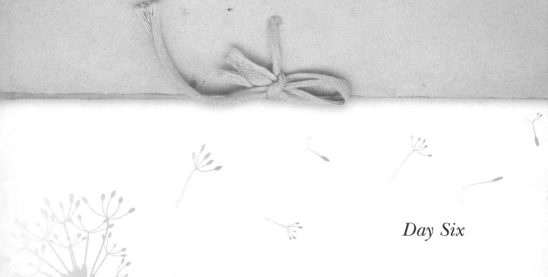

Day Six

THOUGHTS

For as he thinks in his heart, so is he.
—Proverbs 23:7

Discipline #6:

INVEST TIME IN CREATING A HEALTHY THOUGHT LIFE

Just as important as those *who* we let into our inner circles of trust is *what* we allow into our minds. The things we read, see, and listen to all affect our thought life. James 1:27 states, *"Religion that God our Father accepts as pure and faultless is this: to look after orphans and widows in their distress and to keep oneself from being polluted by the world"* (NIV). There is a certain amount of filth in the world that we are going to be exposed to by no choice of our own, but there is a lot we *can* do to guard our minds. It might be counter-cultural, and you could be labeled an "extremist" or "fanatic," but ultimately you'll be living an abundant and resilient life that pleases God.

REFLECTION QUESTIONS

Why is it so important to not be "polluted by the world"?

_____

_____

_____

_____

_____

_____

Are there some media habits you have that are polluting your soul? If so, what are they?

_____

_____

_____

_____

_____

_____

Are you reading/watching/listening to something that gives you temporary pleasure but leaves your mind darkened? If so, which are you willing to give up?

_____

_____

_____

_____

_____

What could be some tough responses from others because you eliminate certain media habits?

_____

_____

_____

_____

How will the benefits outweigh the costs?

_____

_____

_____

_____

_____

ACTIVATION EXERCISE

Make a list of the types of media you are ingesting inadvertently or by choice (TV, movies, music, websites, social media, magazines, advertisements, etc.).

Do this next part with the Holy Spirit: Go through the list and put an "X" by that which might pollute your soul.

Now make a plan with the Holy Spirit's guidance as to how you will avoid those things in the future.

EMPOWERMENT PRAYER

Say this out loud:

Jesus, I am so thankful that Your blood washes away all my filthy stains. Would You wash over me and purify my soul? I don't want to meditate on sinful things. I want to be a pure vessel for Your life and love to flow in and through me to bless the world. I choose to loose ungodly soul ties from media in my life. Thank you, Jesus, for Your resurrection power living inside of me, enabling me to live a pure and holy life.

Day Seven

MINDSETS

*The evil mindset spread to the leaders and
priests and filtered down to the people—
it kicked off an epidemic of evil.*
—2 CHRONICLES 36:14, MSG

Discipline #7:
CAREFULLY EVALUATE ALL THOUGHTS
THAT COME INTO YOUR MIND

As we seek to purify our minds and align them with heaven's perspective, we must guard against being deceived in our mindsets. One way deception can creep in is by the spiritual teaching that we ingest. Unfortunately, not all teachers and pastors who say they believe in Jesus are actually preaching biblical doctrine. How can we know who to listen to? To begin with, they should teach that Jesus is the Son of God and the *only* way we can have a relationship with God and inherit eternal life. They should be living pure and holy lives. If they are living in sin, that will make them vulnerable to deception. There should be evidence of the fruit of the Spirit in their attitudes and behaviors. (See Galatians 5:22-23.) And of course, their teaching should line up with the Word of God, the nature of who God is, and always draw you closer to Jesus.

REFLECTION QUESTIONS

Are you aware of spiritual teachers who appear to be good at first glance, but have teachings that are not biblical?

_____

_____

_____

_____

_____

_____

Where do you get most of your spiritual teaching? (Include your church, books, online teaching, radio, TV, etc.)

_____

_____

_____

_____

_____

_____

Are you confident these spiritual teachers fit the criteria in today's devotional?

ACTIVATION EXERCISE

If you are not sure whether to continue listening to a certain spiritual teacher, do some research; but remember, if you search for information online, you may not get accurate information. People intentionally slander many Christian teachers. Ultimately, your decision of whom to heed must be between you and the Holy Spirit.

EMPOWERMENT PRAYER

Heavenly Father, thank You for giving me the Holy Spirit who leads me into all truth. I want the truth, not a lie, so please keep me from deception. Would You bring wise and godly Christian friends into my life to help me stay in line with the Word of God as well? Would You also alert me when something is off-base with a teacher whom I am learning from so that I don't become deceived? I want to have faith like a child, but also discernment that is as sharp as a tack. Thank you, Holy Spirit.

Day Eight

ATTITUDES

*For you died, and your life is now
hidden with Christ in God.*
—Colossians 3:3, NIV

Discipline #8:
EMBRACE WHO GOD SAYS YOU ARE IN CHRIST

There are a myriad of ways our identities have been shaped or reshaped—our family's social status, the people we associate with, our job, the level of education we have received, the way we dress, the car we drive, the things we own, the place we live, our past experiences (positive or negative), etc. However, we can choose to agree or disagree with the labels that come from these things. The truth is that in Christ we are a new creation. Our true and authentic image comes from the knowledge that we are sons or daughters of God. Unless we renew our mind with the truth of who God says we are, we are susceptible to living with identities that do not reflect our true identity in Christ.

REFLECTION QUESTIONS

Do you tend to identify more with who the world says you are, or who God says you are?

_____

_____

_____

_____

_____

_____

_____

What is the biggest pull or contributing factor that has caused you to view yourself as you do today?

_____

_____

_____

_____

_____

_____

_____

_____

Ask the Holy Spirit to help you identify any lies you are believing about yourself—or any labels you are falsely wearing.

_____

_____

_____

_____

_____

Now, ask Him what the truth is.

_____

_____

_____

_____

Take a moment to ask God if there is anything more He wants you to shift or adjust regarding how you see yourself.

_____

_____

_____

_____

_____

Activation Exercises

On the scale below, mark how confident you feel with your identity in Christ.

0%	10%	20%	30%	40%	50%	60%	70%	80%	90%	100%

Make an action plan to become more secure with who you are in Christ. Ideas may include putting verses and declarations about who God says you are in visible places, reminding yourself of God's love at specified times throughout the day, listening to uplifting songs about your identity, or creating a piece of art to hang in your workplace or residence to remind yourself of who you are in Christ.

Mark your calendar to revisit this in thirty days to see whether your confidence in your identity in Christ has increased.

Empowerment Prayer

Heavenly Father, thank You for loving me and calling me Your beloved son/daughter. I want to see myself as You see me. Would You help me drop the false labels that I have associated with myself, and replace them with the truth of who You say I am in Christ? I choose to come into agreement with the fact that I am a beloved child of God. Please help me to more fully embrace my true identity. Amen.

Day Nine

BELIEFS

No prolonged infancies among us, please. We'll not tolerate babes in the woods, small children who are an easy mark for impostors. God wants us to grow up, to know the whole truth and tell it in love—like Christ in everything.
—Ephesians 4:14-15, MSG

Discipline #9:
DELIBERATELY FORM YOUR BELIEF SYSTEM

On Day Seven we discussed being cautious about where you get your spiritual teaching. Today we'll talk more about how your belief system is formed. Perhaps you find a teacher you are confident is reading the Word, has a close relationship with Jesus, is walking in purity and holiness, and has evidence of the fruit of the Spirit in their life; but no matter who they are, they are still growing (hopefully). The best teachers and leaders are continuously growing in their beliefs and how they apply the Word, just as much as you or me. Therefore, you shouldn't place 100 percent of your confidence in one person's teaching alone. Your confidence should ultimately be in the Bible and in discerning God's voice for yourself. After all, it is the truth that *you* know and are intimately acquainted with that sets you free (see John 8:32).

REFLECTION QUESTIONS

How have your beliefs changed over the years?

_____

_____

_____

_____

_____

Have you noticed your favorite spiritual teacher's beliefs change over time?

_____

_____

_____

_____

_____

_____

_____

_____

_____

_____

_____

_____

Do you turn your brain off when you listen to or read messages from your favorite teacher? A clue would be whether or not you agree with everything they say, or whether you search the truth out in the Bible for yourself (see 2 Tim. 2:15; Acts 17:11).

_____

_____

_____

How can you rely more on what the Bible and the Holy Spirit say, rather than solely on what a person teaches?

_____

_____

_____

_____

_____

_____

_____

_____

ACTIVATION EXERCISES

Ask the Holy Spirit if there are any beliefs about God you hold that are not true. If you hear "yes," ask Him what they are.

Now ask Him to reveal to you what the truth is—and then check to make sure it lines up with scripture.

EMPOWERMENT PRAYER

Dear Lord, forgive me for times that I have relied more on what people say I should believe rather than what You say. I want to hear Your voice and truth above all else. Help me to listen carefully—with my heart, head, and spirit— as I absorb new teaching. Help me not to place too much emphasis on certain beliefs that aren't that important in Your sight. I want to believe what is true with the proper perspective and emphasis. You're the best teacher!

Day Ten

PARADIGMS

Since you have been raised to new life with Christ, set your sights on the realities of heaven, where Christ sits in the place of honor at God's right hand. Think about the things of heaven, not the things of earth. For you died to this life, and your real life is hidden with Christ in God.
—COLOSSIANS 3:1-3, NLT

Discipline #10:
MAINTAIN A KINGDOM PERSPECTIVE

The way that we operate on a daily basis, the way that we live life, all stems from our paradigms—the way we process information and our pattern of thinking. The keys to living a successful and victorious life are found in the underpinnings of our foundational paradigms. What we believe about God, what we believe about ourselves, and what we believe about the world and other people are all very much intertwined. For instance, when we have a tainted view of God, we see ourselves and the world around us through a lens that falsely misrepresents everything that we see.

Maintaining a perspective that is heaven bound instead of earth bound helps to clear our lens of the things that tend to otherwise cloud our vision.

REFLECTION QUESTIONS

In what way do you live from a place of negative thinking?

_____

_____

_____

_____

_____

_____

_____

How does this affect your daily life? Your walk with the Lord? Your relationships?

_____

_____

_____

_____

_____

_____

_____

What do you think it looks like to be heavenly-minded?

How can you actively pursue shifting your mindset from being self focused to kingdom focused?

ACTIVATION EXERCISES

Ask the Holy Spirit to show you where your perspective needs to be readjusted. Write out the specific paradigms that you would like to work on. Find scripture verses to meditate on that will help you reverse negative ways of thinking.

EMPOWERMENT PRAYER

Lord, teach me to be heavenly-minded. Open my eyes to see the way You do, that I might walk in the fullness of Christ. I want to be someone who sees with a kingdom perspective and is a conduit for Your purposes on the earth. Give me the strength I need to fulfill Your purpose for me every moment of every day. Thank You for giving me the tools I need to operate in a paradigm that rightly reflects who You are. Amen.

Day Eleven

WE VERSUS ME

That there may be no division in the body, but that the
members may have the same care for one another.
—1 Corinthians 12:25, ESV

Discipline #11:
BE "WE-MINDED" INSTEAD OF "ME-MINDED"

One the most valuable things we have in life are the people
who fill it. There are two very basic kinds of relationships: Type
One—those motivated by self, and Type Two—those motivated
by love. Type One relationships are made up of individuals who
are only involved for their own benefit; this is clearly destructive to a relationship on any level. Type Two relationships are
comprised of individuals who provide support, encouragement,
camaraderie, etc. and expect nothing in return. The latter,
of course, is the healthy, kingdom-based relationship. It isn't
always easy, and it takes honesty, trust, and humility on the part

of both parties to create authentic Type Two relationships. The qualities of a kingdom-based relationship, however, will always produce lasting fruit and life.

REFLECTION QUESTIONS

Consider the various relationships in your life. Are these relationships motivated by love for self or by love for another?

_____

_____

_____

_____

_____

_____

_____

What are the qualities that you value most in your relationships?

_____

_____

_____

_____

_____

_____

_____

_____

_____

_____

_____

_____

_____

_____

_____

Do you reciprocate these qualities in your respective relationships?

_____

_____

_____

_____

_____

_____

_____

_____

_____

_____

ACTIVATION EXERCISES

Ask the Lord to show you what relationships in your life could be, or need to be, approached differently. Take a moment to search your heart and let the Holy Spirit speak to you. Make an action plan. List the character qualities you need to develop to improve the quality of your most valued relationships.

EMPOWERMENT PRAYER

Jesus, make me a person of humility who is not self-seeking. Teach me to be selfless in my relationships that I would give freely in love, without needing or wanting anything in return. Lord, I want to be like You. Purify my heart that I might walk in love just like You did. Root out any wrong expectations that I may have in my current relationships, or any wounds carried over from past ones. Make me a person who is a fountain of life for others, so that I can create a place for long-lasting and meaningful relationships. Amen.

Day Twelve

JUST VERSUS UNJUST

*Walk straight, act right, tell the truth. Don't hurt your
friend, don't blame your neighbor; despise the despicable.*
—Psalms 15:2-4, MSG

Discipline #12:
VALUE SERVICE OVER SELFISHNESS

Unhealthy soul ties at their root are born from dysfunctional
or broken relationships. Healthy relationships take a lot of
intentionality and personal character growth—on the part
of all parties—to maintain. Relationships require hard work
whether they involve family, friends, or a significant other. If
we truly value our relationships, we will do whatever is necessary to make them work. Oftentimes, this involves the low road
of humility.

Jesus left us an example of servanthood when it comes to
how He operated in His own relationships. He modeled the

servant heart of a king when sitting with sinners, looking after His followers, or washing His disciple's feet. God, in human skin, was selfless! How much more should we endeavor to put others' needs before our own? The heart of a true friend is never self-seeking.

REFLECTION QUESTIONS

How are your actions and behaviors honoring of other people?

_____

_____

_____

_____

_____

_____

_____

When it comes to your most precious relationships, does your behavior toward and response to them reflect how Jesus might have behaved or responded?

_____

_____

_____

_____

_____

_____

_____

_____

_____

_____

_____

Are you the first to extend grace, or are you quick to take offense?

_____

_____

_____

_____

_____

_____

_____

_____

_____

_____

_____

_____

ACTIVATION EXERCISES

Ask the Lord to show you where you can grow as an individual in your respective relationships. Ask Him for His heart and His perspective, and to give you the wisdom and grace you need to be a person of humility and integrity in every area.

EMPOWERMENT PRAYER

Dear Lord, thank You for each relationship that You have brought into my life. Thank You for family, leaders, mentors, and faithful friends. God, I ask that You would teach me to be more mindful of others, that I would learn to honor and esteem those You've placed around me. Give me a heart like Yours that I would be a servant just as You were. Give me wisdom to know how best to serve and the grace to walk in it. Amen.

Day Thirteen

INTERDEPENDENCE VERSUS INDEPENDENCE

*The human body has many parts, but the many parts
make up only one body. So it is with the body of Christ.*
—1 CORINTHIANS 12:12, NLT

Discipline #13:
PURSUE INTEGRATION OVER ISOLATION

We are all created with the innate desire to belong and to be connected to something bigger than ourselves. But in searching for this fulfillment, we get disappointed and become bitter toward people, the Church, etc., causing most of us to resort to a lifestyle of independence—thinking we are better off on our own because people can't be trusted. Isolation is a breeding ground for dysfunction both within an individual and all those with whom they relate. It is the polar opposite of what Christ desires for us.

The kingdom of God is built upon the principle of interdependence—like any healthy organism, the whole is always greater than the sum of its parts. It requires synergy to make any system work. Much like the human body, the Body of Christ is a highly interconnected ecosystem, community, or family. It takes some breaking down of each member's personal walls and defenses for all to become vulnerable enough to "know and be known" in order for the community to thrive. It takes trust.

Every individual has something important to offer the whole, and in making that offering, each will find the enrichment, vitality, and meaning that results in an abundant life. This is why Jesus likens the Church to a *body*. The Body needs you as much as you need the Body. Think how much less abundant your life would be without your church—that's how much less your church would be without you! Believe it, because it is true.

You matter.

REFLECTION QUESTIONS

Do you belong to a community, organization, or group where you are able to connect with a larger vision?

_____

_____

_____

_____

_____

_____

How do you add value, and how does that add value to you?

_____

_____

_____

_____

_____

_____

Do you have isolative tendencies?

_____

_____

If so, what steps can you take to more frequently connect with people on a personal level?

_____

_____

_____

_____

_____

_____

_____

ACTIVATION EXERCISES

Ask the Holy Spirit to reveal places in your life where you are more independent than interdependent, where you have become isolated and emotionally detached or cut off from people. Let Him walk you through the emotional scars that have caused you to mistrust people and isolate yourself. Are you remembering or seeing specific instances in your past? Let Him bring restoration to the broken places of your heart.

EMPOWERMENT PRAYER

Lord, teach me the significance and importance of being an integral part of the Body of Christ. Give me a revelation of the power of unity in the Church and the important part that I play in it. I thank You that I don't have to live life alone and isolated from the world. Instead, You have given me a family and body of people to walk with me. Thank You, God, that You are good, and You meet my every need.

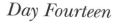

Day Fourteen

"CONTENDING FOR" VERSUS "COMPETING WITH"

Agree with each other, love each other, be deep-spirited friends. Don't push your way to the front; don't sweet-talk your way to the top. Put yourself aside, and help others get ahead. Don't be obsessed with getting your own advantage.
—Philippians 2:2-4, MSG

Discipline #14:
CONTEND FOR RATHER THAN COMPETE WITH OTHERS

In group settings, especially among family, we can fall into a competitive mode without even realizing it. In doing this, we lose sight of each other's true value and the importance of coming alongside one another to contend for our mutual success. True Christ-likeness is being able to celebrate others' strengths and successes. This takes humility and a sense of confidence in the God who created each of us to bring our uniqueness to bear on the world. A mark of maturity is not only to have confidence in one's own abilities, but also in the abilities of others. Rejoicing in the success of another should be a natural response where relationships are life-giving and healthy (see Rom. 12:3-13).

REFLECTION QUESTIONS

Are you able to look upon the success of others positively?

_____

_____

_____

_____

_____

Do you have a hidden desire to see others fail?

_____

_____

If so, what keeps you from rejoicing or contending for another's massive success?

_____

_____

_____

_____

Why do you think you react this way?

What might change in your own life if you truly contended for the success of those around you?

ACTIVATION EXERCISES

Ask the Lord to reveal the hidden things in your heart—the hidden motives that even you can't see. Allow Him to show you the deep things that keep you from being able to fully contend for the success of others. Make a conscious effort to stay in a place of thankfulness, keeping your thoughts centered on a heavenly perspective.

EMPOWERMENT PRAYER

Lord, I ask that You would soften my heart, mold me into a person who bears an unmistakable Christ-likeness. I want to be a person who rejoices with those who rejoice, and is able to come alongside others to contend for the fulfillment of Your promises in every area of their lives. Give me a heart of understanding that I may walk in love and compassion when it is needed most. Amen.

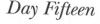

Day Fifteen

WIN-WIN VERSUS WIN-LOSE

And if one member suffers, all the members
suffer with it; or if one member is honored,
all the members rejoice with it.
—1 Corinthians 12:26

Discipline #15:
CHOOSE TO ADD VALUE TO
EVERY RELATIONSHIP

What does a relationship that "adds value" look like? Essentially, it is a relationship that is mutually beneficial to everyone involved. This type of relationship seeks the good and believes the best of the other person; it is sacrificial, it is win-win, and it is empowering. These types of relationships might be with those people who have walked through the fire with you, or with a newer relationship you are cultivating and hoping to graft into a circle of trust. These kinds of friendships—both personal and professional—are the treasured gold we have this side of eternity.

When we find in Jesus all that we need for fulfillment, we eradicate the need for competition, or the pursuit of our own self-based needs in the context of our relationships. Kingdom-focused relationships build up all involved while strengthening and undergirding who He has called each of us to be. We are each but a product of the quality of our relationships. As the character Sherlock Holmes, from the popular TV show *Elementary*, was quoted as saying, "I feel I've thrived here not because of who I am, but because of who I've come to know."

REFLECTION QUESTIONS

Think about the long-term friendships in your life. What specifically is it about these relationships that creates longevity?

_____

_____

_____

_____

_____

_____

Do you feel that they reciprocate that same kind of strength-building element that you give to them?

_____

_____

_____

What do you feel is lacking from your relationships, and why?

Activation Exercises

In Christ we have all we will ever need. We lack nothing. He has seen your life from its beginning to its end, and has not overlooked a single detail! Ask Him to fill the places where you feel you are lacking. Write down those specific needs, and be honest. Look at the areas of disappointment; why do feel that Jesus is not enough? Which lies are you believing about the nature of God? How has this affected your relationships? How might knowledge of the truth add value to them?

Empowerment Prayer

God, I thank You that You are all-sufficient; that You take me just as I am, without question. Thank You that You never leave me empty-handed, that heaven is available here on earth—all we have to do is ask! So Father, I'm asking that You fill me right now, and give me the ability to see through Your eyes, that I might be able to release Your kingdom here on earth to those in my sphere of influence. Amen.

Day Sixteen

THE DYNAMICS OF DYSFUNCTION

Even now the axe is laid to the root of the trees.
—Matthew 3:10, ESV

Discipline #16:
DEAL WITH THE ROOT TO CHANGE THE FRUIT

The majority, if not all, of the problems you face go deeper than what you see on the surface. Similar to a tree, which is secured by roots that run far beneath the visible surface, so it is with the emotions and different elements of your soul. "Bad" roots create dysfunctional thought patterns, habits, and relationships. In order to "unbind" this root system, it must be uncovered and dealt with as a gardener would "de-weed" or address the health of the soil beneath a garden—by removing any visible weeds by their invisible roots. When the garden is free of weeds, it will flourish.

Our lives flourish when our relationships flourish. The quality of the fruit we bear is evidenced by the quality of our relationships. When our relationships are fruitful in all areas, we are fruitful in all areas. This is the foundation for success and prosperity (see Matt. 7:17-19; 12:35), so it is vital that we look closely and assess the kind of fruit we are bearing.

REFLECTION QUESTIONS

What kind of fruit are you bearing in your life?

_____

_____

_____

_____

_____

_____

_____

Where might you need to do some weeding?

_____

_____

_____

_____

_____

_____

How will this affect those closest to you?

_____

_____

_____

_____

_____

_____

_____

_____

How could this change the dynamics of your various circles of trust?

_____

_____

_____

_____

_____

_____

_____

_____

ACTIVATION EXERCISES

Take a moment to examine your heart. Ask the Holy Spirit to show you the roots of any dysfunction. Let Him walk you through past experiences that have allowed these things to be cultivated in your life. Where is it coming from? What actions do you need to take to remove these tendencies? Are there individuals you need to talk it through with? Don't be afraid to ask for help! If you have pastors, leaders, mentors, or friends who speak into your life, it's important to have people come alongside you in the healing process.

EMPOWERMENT PRAYER

Lord, I want to bear good fruit! Strip away everything that keeps me from walking in wholeness and health. I recognize that I need You to help me walk through this process, to show me the changes I must make, and to do the deeper work of healing. Give me the grace and the strength I need to uproot the things in my life that keep me from making healthy choices. Jesus, I trust Your leadership, and I trust that You are here with me even now. Amen.

Day Seventeen

THE DE-MOTIVATOR
OF SHAME

*Because the Sovereign Lord helps me, I will
not be disgraced. Therefore, I have set my face
like a stone, determined to do his will. And
I know that I will not be put to shame.*
—Isaiah 50:7, NLT

Discipline #17:
FOCUS ON ISSUES, NOT INDIVIDUALS

We often avoid the crux of an issue by pointing the finger at
an individual—or take attention off of ourselves, and the real
problem, by blaming and shaming someone else. Instead of
creating an avenue to solve problems, this only leads to more
damage. In order to heal relationships and the broken pieces

in between, we have to get to the heart of the issue and uncover it; this will bring healing in its wake.

Shame is a master emotional manipulator, which makes a slave out of everyone it touches. Shame seeks to conceal and control until the whole of our identity is wrapped up in something that is completely contrary to who Jesus says we are. In order to break this vicious cycle, it is vital that we understand who we are in His sight. We must counter shame by embracing our own divine nature, revealing the hope of glory that resides in us (see 2 Pet. 1:4; Col. 1:27).

REFLECTION QUESTIONS

Are you operating in shame unknowingly?

_____

_____

_____

_____

What areas of your life are rooted in shame?

_____

_____

_____

_____

How is this affecting your relationships? Did you grow up in a shame-based home or community?

_____

_____

Who specifically made you feel ashamed?

How has this stunted your personal and professional growth? How has it kept you from forming healthy relationships?

How has it prevented you from being truly happy?

Activation Exercises

God does not want you to be overcome with shame. It's not how He created you to live, and it does not reflect the price Jesus paid for you on the cross. Ask the Holy Spirit to take you back to where it all started. Let Him walk you through those moments and show you where He was then—and where He is now.

Empowerment Prayer

Dear Lord, forgive me for walking in this identity of shame. I break every agreement with the spirit of shame, and I refuse to partner with this any longer. You paid the highest price for me so that I would have the ability to walk in freedom and embrace the identity You designed just for me. Thank You that I no longer have to walk in shame or condemnation, and that I am seated with You in heavenly places! Father, thank You for making all things new, and leave nothing undone. Amen.

Day Eighteen

WHEN HELPING YOU IS HURTING ME

The righteous should choose his friends carefully,
for the way of the wicked leads them astray.
—PROVERBS 12:26

Discipline #18:
RESIST YIELDING TO THE CONTROL OF OTHERS

Relationships can be complicated and messy sometimes. I am sure we all have experienced this to some degree. There are those that give us great joy and strengthen us, and there are others that are harmful. The most detrimental of all relationships are those that are co-dependent. This particular type of relationship can take many forms. Ultimately, what it comes down to are two emotionally unstable and unhealthy individuals who cannot break away from each other because they have created an "I need you to need me" relationship. One needs to depend and the other needs to be depended upon.

Every one of us can and should help friends and family members, but when help turns into a cycle of enablement followed by emotional or physical pain, that is a sign of dysfunction. Many of us get entangled in co-dependency by reaching out to someone out of sheer compassion, but then that rescuing behavior turns into a cycle where we are unable to say "no" to unrealistic demands. This is proof that an unhealthy soul tie exists. When boundaries are violated and helping benefits only one of the parties involved, it is time to reassess the nature of the relationship to determine if it should be healed or severed.

REFLECTION QUESTIONS

Are you involved in a relationship that you feel unnecessarily bound to?

_____

_____

Who is the benefactor in the relationship? Whose needs are being met?

_____

_____

_____

Are you being mentally or physically abused?

_____

_____

_____

_____

_____

_____

Are you being taken advantage of financially or emotionally?

_____

_____

_____

_____

_____

Is this a relationship the Lord wants you to invest in and work through? Or is this a relationship you need to walk away from?

_____

_____

_____

_____

_____

_____

_____

_____

_____

Activation Exercises

As you reflect on the questions above, think about your level of involvement. What is your motivation in the relationship? Are you being moved by compassion or bound by guilt? If the answer is the latter, ask the Lord how to move forward. If you need to, take a moment to develop a plan, write a letter, or make a phone call to the particular individual(s). Do whatever is necessary to maintain healthy boundaries in your life.

Empowerment Prayer

Lord, thank You that You have given me a sound mind. I ask that You would give me the wisdom to make healthy choices, that I would have the grace to make changes in my relationships where needed. I want to know Your heart. God, I ask that You would give me peace in the process and the courage to do what's right.

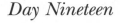

Day Nineteen

SPIRITUAL DIMENSIONS
OF RELATIONSHIPS

The thief comes only to steal and kill and destroy.
—John 10:10, ESV

Discipline #19:
DISCERN THE SPIRITUAL RAMIFICATIONS
OF ALL YOUR RELATIONSHIPS

As we have been discussing, being aware and assessing the possible detriments of different relationships helps to keep our discernment in tune. When we avoid facing the problems at hand, it gives them control over us. The enemy's most powerful weapon is ignorance and complacency. Too many don't fully realize that not dealing with unhealthy relationships will affect all areas of their life—from their emotional and physical health to their spiritual health.

All facets and dimensions of our being are interrelated. There are spiritual things happening all around us, every moment of every day, that go unnoticed by our natural senses. In the same way, our relationships have spiritual dimensions that have causes and effects in our lives—much more than we know—the ramifications of which can be devastating if left to play out unhindered. History itself is evidence of this. Hence, it is absolutely necessary that we are aware of what we may be fighting against or inadvertently partnering with. (For more on this topic, see my book, *The Rules of Engagement for Spiritual Battles*.)

REFLECTION QUESTIONS

Do you feel like you are "battling heavily" in the spirit with certain relationships?

_____

_____

_____

_____

_____

_____

Do you know of dark spiritual things taking place with any of the individuals in your life, such as witchcraft, suicidal thoughts, mental/psychiatric conditions, etc.?

_____

_____

_____

If so, consider how involved with this person you may be, and what ramifications this might have for you.

ACTIVATION EXERCISES

Just because you care about someone doesn't mean you need to dabble in his or her life choices. When you think about different dynamics and people you are in relationship with, does anything stand out to you as a red flag? Ask the Holy Spirit to point out anything you might be affected by as a result of someone else's personal choices.

EMPOWERMENT PRAYER

Lord, I ask for greater discernment, that You would give me a greater depth of understanding to see with open eyes the things of the spirit. Help me to make choices that will benefit and not harm me in the future. Father, I also ask that You would help me to love people in my life rightly, without getting caught up in circumstances that will create a harmful chain reaction. You are the God of all wisdom, so Lord I trust that You will lead me and guide me in all truth.

Day Twenty

KEEP WATCH!

Stay alert! Watch out for your great enemy,
the devil. He prowls around like a roaring
lion, looking for someone to devour.
—1 Peter 5:8, NLT

Discipline #20:
NEVER LET YOUR GUARD DOWN

When we experience healing or deliverance in a certain area, it is vital that we keep a watchful eye and maintain the ground that has been conquered. When we are not watchful, we become vulnerable and unknowingly give the enemy access to regain the places where he has once had a foothold in our lives. We must be careful not to allow him any room for re-entry. The necessary steps for this will look different for everyone. It will entail setting personal standards and raising the bar in areas you may have compromised previously. To help you with this, it is necessary to establish a healthy relationship with the Spirit of God and become familiar with His still, small voice. If you do nothing else in this life, learn to be led by the Holy Spirit (see John 16:13; Isa.11:2).

REFLECTION QUESTIONS

What steps can you take to more closely follow the leading of the Holy Spirit?

_____

_____

_____

_____

_____

_____

_____

What would you like to see yourself do differently?

_____

_____

_____

_____

_____

_____

_____

Knowing what you know now, what boundaries will you set in place to keep from returning to unhealthy relationship patterns?

Activation Exercises

If you have just come out of a dysfunctional relationship and are looking to make a new start, you've got to have a plan of action to keep yourself moving forward. Are there trustworthy leaders/people in your life who can hold you accountable, who you can be 100 percent honest with? Write these names down. Pray about asking if they would be a person of accountability in your life as you continue to walk this out.

Empowerment Prayer

Lord, thank You for all that You are doing in my life. Thank You that You are a God of redemption and new life. You have given me beyond what I could ever think or ask; You are abounding in mercy. In the coming days, I ask that You help me hear Your voice and follow where You lead. I need Your help to continue this journey of healing and to walk in wisdom. Amen.

PURSUE DESTINY-DEFINING MOMENTS

For everyone who asks receives; the one who seeks finds;
and to the one who knocks, the door will be opened.
—MATTHEW 7:8, NIV

Discipline #21:
SEEK LIFE-GIVING RELATIONSHIPS

Having covenant friendships in your life is essential to walking in what God has called you to. God uses people of all different sizes, shapes, and colors to speak to you and to steer you toward your divine destiny. The names we remember throughout history rarely succeeded alone; most had family, friends, teams of leaders, or just a handful of committed comrades who walked with them to carry out their dreams and visions. To try and do it on your own is only setting yourself up for failure.

God wants you to have healthy relationships. He has designed certain relationships to be the catalysts that launch you into what He has ordained for your life. Look for and cultivate relationships that will stabilize and strengthen you. Surround yourself with those you can lock arms with. You never know what destiny-defining moments these relationships will position you to step into!

REFLECTION QUESTIONS

Although you may not do so consciously, what are the specific characteristics you look for in friendships?

_____

_____

_____

_____

_____

_____

_____

What kind of personality traits are you drawn to? Which turn you off?

_____

_____

_____

_____

_____

What type of temperament compliments yours?

How might your current relationships move you toward—or away from—your destiny?

Activation Exercises

What drives you? We all have strengths and we all have weaknesses. Often our greatest weakness is tied to our greatest strength. Your weaknesses don't define you, however, nor do they have to limit you. Partner with people who can compensate for your weak areas and compliment your strengths.

Empowerment Prayer

Dear Lord, thank You for creating us to work together. I ask that You bring people into my life who would stand beside me, walk with me on this journey, and help guide me into the destiny You have planned for me. Thank You, Lord, for bringing healthy and life-giving relationships into my life in the coming days. I ask that I would be open and receptive even to unlikely voices of wisdom. Guide my steps and help me to walk in Your ways. Amen.

Day Twenty-Two

PURSUE A RENEWED MIND

Be renewed in the spirit of your mind.
—Ephesians 4:23

Discipline #22:
REPLACE NEGATIVE MINDSETS
WITH GOD'S TRUTH

Our mind is often referred to as our greatest battleground. It is the stage where we fight some of our fiercest battles—and why being armed with Truth is of such grave importance. If we are fighting a battle with misinformation and negative mindsets, we have already lost! However, God has given us a ready and available weapon—His Word.

There is power in the living Word of God to infuse our minds with new ways of thinking. In order to win the war in our thought lives, we must continually meditate on the Truth found in scripture, daily renew our minds with the promises of

God, and speak those promises over the circumstances of our lives. Make this a daily practice if you haven't already. Be intentional about disciplining yourself to read your Bible every day, memorize scripture, and speak it out—you will begin to see a change in the way you think and the way you experience life.

REFLECTION QUESTIONS

In the past, what lies have you believed?

_____

_____

_____

_____

_____

_____

Why did you believe these to be true?

_____

_____

_____

_____

_____

_____

_____

What mental battle are you currently fighting?

What are the weapons you need to overcome?

ACTIVATION EXERCISES

Find scriptures that declare the opposite of the lies you have believed about yourself or your circumstances. Write these scriptures out on note cards and place them throughout your home, or in prominent places where you will see them on a daily basis to remind you of what God says. When breaking free of destructive soul ties, it is essential that you replace what you *break* with what you *build*. As you break free from what is false, you must build upon what is true!

EMPOWERMENT PRAYER

Lord, thank You for giving me Your Word as a weapon of truth. It declares what I have, and it reveals who I am. You have given me all I need to reverse the mindsets that have kept me from fully walking in the fullness of Your promises for my life. I thank You that You have good things in store for me, and You are intricately connected to the smallest details of my life. You see my past, my failures, my present, and the destiny You have called me to; You will complete the good work You've begun in me. Help me to stand on the unwavering truth of Your Word. Amen.

Day Twenty-Three

PURSUE JOY

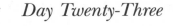

Rejoice in the Lord always. Again I will say, rejoice!
—Philippians 4:4

Discipline #23:
SEEK ACTIVITIES AND PEOPLE
WHO MAKE YOU COME ALIVE

Living life from a place of joy allows us to live independent from circumstances or things we may encounter on a daily basis. It is a choice. We cannot wait around until we feel joy to *be* joyful. Often, when breaking free from soul ties, we feel as though we are losing our sense of identity and, in turn, experience depression and sadness. Why? So much of who we thought we were was attached to another person, belief, idea, paradigm, or circumstance. I encourage you during this journey to reclaiming your soul—make the choice to rejoice! (See Philippians 4:4-8.) Within this choice resides incredible freedom.

One of the greatest keys to living a life of joy is that of thankfulness. When you are able to look at your life and live in gratitude for both the greatest and smallest of blessings, even for the challenges, it creates a platform for God to bring more blessing into your life.

Gratitude is akin to wonder, and wonder feeds our creativity. Pursuing creativity is a way to both glorify God and rejoice in what is possible. Stir your passion by finding ways to creatively express yourself. It will greatly enhance your life! Remember, joy is a choice. Oftentimes, it involves us positioning ourselves around people and in environments where joy can be cultivated.

REFLECTION QUESTIONS

If you could do absolutely anything in the world, what would you do?

_____

_____

_____

_____

_____

_____

What is the one thing that makes you come alive when you do it?

_____

_____

_____

_____

What have you dreamed about doing and becoming?

What measurable steps can you take to pursue fulfilling these dreams? How else can you bring joy to your life?

Activation Exercises

Begin making steps toward joy. You can do this by writing out a list of the top ten things you are thankful for (and more if you'd like) and why you are thankful for them. Thank God for each of these things first thing in the morning for the next seven days, and watch how it changes your perspective.

Empowerment Prayer

God, thank You for Your unchanging goodness. Thank You for every blessing You've given me, even for the things that I often take for granted. You are the author of life itself, and because of all You have done for me, I can live a joy-filled life! Lord, I ask that You would help me live from a grateful heart and approach every day with joy, not weighed down by the cares or concerns of this world. Help me to be mindful of all that You've done for me, and all that You continue to do. Amen.

Day Twenty-Four

PURSUE PURPOSE

*Look carefully then how you walk! Live purposefully
and worthily and accurately, not as the unwise and
witless, but as wise (sensible, intelligent people).*
—Ephesians 5:15, AMP

Discipline #24:
LIVE INTENTIONALLY

If you plan to live a resilient life and become all that God has
created you to be, it will take commitment and intentionality. Intention causes people to show up for work every day to
advance someone else's agenda and purpose—yet those same
people rarely show up for their own lives to advance their own
agenda and purpose. Just as you intentionally show up for work
every Monday, show up for your own life and be intentional
about it. Intentionally pursue your own God-given purpose and

maximize your own divine potential. Intentionally get rid of self-defeating habits and undermining relationships.

Like a person who has gained mastery over their craft, you must gain mastery over your life. Take your life out of neutral. No one can make this commitment for you. During this 40-day period you will encounter many obstacles and be tempted to abandon these daily disciplines. You may even reach the point of wanting to give up, or feel that there are other things preventing you from completing this wonderfully enriching and empowering experience. Intend to finish and you will. All of heaven will conspire with earth to make sure you do.

REFLECTION QUESTIONS

What do you feel is your specific purpose?

_____

_____

_____

_____

_____

_____

_____

What has God called you to?

_____

_____

_____

_____

_____

_____

What causes you feel His pleasure when you do it?

_____

_____

_____

_____

Are you taking steps right now toward doing these things? If not, why?

_____

_____

_____

_____

What can you do to more intentionally pursue your goals, dreams, and desires?

_____

_____

_____

_____

_____

_____

Activation Exercises

Consider for a moment what you spend the majority of your time doing. Is it work-related? Is it something you enjoy doing?

Make a list of what you would like to accomplish in the next six months to a year. The next three years. The next five years. The next ten years. Be specific.

Write a specific start date and completion date next to each goal.

Which do you intend to make a reality?

Empowerment Prayer

Dear Lord, thank You for all of the gifts, dreams, and desires You've placed within me. Help me to use my time wisely and efficiently. I want my life to be a reflection of Your worthiness. Help me to more intentionally cultivate the things You've placed within my heart to do. I want to be one who faithfully stewards what You've placed in my hands; thank You for guiding my heart and directing my steps. Amen.

Day Twenty-Five

PURSUE GOD'S PRESENCE

Now the Lord is the Spirit, and where
the Spirit of the Lord is, there is liberty
(emancipation from bondage, freedom).
—2 Corinthians 3:17, AMP

Discipline #25:
CREATE AN ATMOSPHERE CHARGED
BY GOD'S PRESENCE

Life at its best can be overwhelming. Through sheer emotional, physical, and psychological exhaustion, we often lose sight of this truth—the presence of God is all around us. We simply get engrossed in what is in front of us, what we see with our physical eyes or experience with our other physical senses. In today's age, our attention is easily captivated by everything *but* God. To live a life of freedom, we must learn to hone our spiritual senses, to become people who are aware of His presence and are acquainted with His nearness. Why? Because when we know how to access the presence of God, it changes everything. It creates an atmosphere of peace, favor, joy, freedom, and blessing.

Remember, God is in all things at all times in all places. There is no place, circumstance, or situation where He is not present. As Christians, we have access to the presence of God every moment of every day, yet so often we don't acknowledge it. Learn to slow down, recognize His nearness, and invite His presence to transform every area of your life. The presence of God is the place of access to a life of breakthrough.

REFLECTION QUESTIONS

What are you most captivated by in life?

_____

_____

_____

_____

_____

_____

_____

_____

What realities are you most aware of—the natural, more temporal realm, or the more supernatural, eternal realm? What do you notice about each?

_____

_____

_____

_____

_____

_____

_____

_____

_____

_____

How might this affect or enhance your ability to fellowship with God and encounter His presence on a daily basis?

_____

_____

_____

_____

_____

_____

_____

_____

_____

ACTIVATION EXERCISES

Set aside 15-30 minutes. Put on some instrumental or worship music, get comfortable, and open your spirit to the presence of God. Whether this is something you are very familiar with, or doing for the first time, just relax and invite God's Spirit to be present. Think about His goodness. Dwell in His perfect peace, unconditional love, and fullness of joy (see Ps. 16:11). Thank Him for His presence. This is the presence we are to carry with us every moment of every day.

EMPOWERMENT PRAYER

Thank You, God, for the gift of Your presence. In it we find all we need and desire in life. Give me an appetite for Your presence—that it would be something I crave more than any earthly thing. Teach me what it is to behold Your beauty and how to carry it with me into every encounter and situation. Your presence is the place of true freedom, so I ask that You give me a greater awareness of your nearness that I might learn to live from a heavenly perspective, empowered and free.

VALUE BOUNDARIES

But let your "Yes" be "Yes," and your "No," "No."
—MATTHEW 5:37

Discipline #26:
MAKE YOUR BOUNDARIES CLEAR AND KNOWN

Having clear boundaries reveals that you value yourself enough to say "no"—and possess the integrity to have firm convictions and stand by your word. By doing so, you tell others you have your own voice and you are not easily swayed by the opinions of other people. It is a very attractive characteristic in both men and women, and it is a foundational quality of emotional stability and health.

As we have learned, words are an exceedingly powerful weapon; they have the ability to release life or death. Boundaries themselves are dictated both by words and by actions. The ability to follow through on what is presented as a boundary line is what will substantiate it and bring it definition. The inability to set boundaries and stick to them, on the other hand, creates an open door for dysfunctional relationships—and the lingering, soul-depleting presence of soul ties. Therefore, we have to be able and *willing* to walk it out once boundaries are set in place.

REFLECTION QUESTIONS

Are you a person of conviction? Do you stand by your word? (This is fundamental to setting boundaries.)

_____

_____

_____

_____

_____

_____

What kind of boundaries do you have in your life? Are they producing the desired result, or do you find people still crossing them?

_____

_____

_____

_____

_____

_____

If you are still experiencing defeat in establishing clear boundaries, what do you think the problem is?

_____

_____

_____

_____

_____

_____

_____

ACTIVATION EXERCISES

Make a list of five boundaries you might set with a close friend.

1. _____

2. _____

3. _____

4. _____

5. _____

Make a list of five boundaries you would set with an acquaintance or co-worker.

1. _____

2. _____

3. _____

4. _____

5. _____

Make a list of five boundaries you'd like to set with a particular family member.

1. _____

2. _____

3. _____

4. _____

5. _____

Choose one from each category you will begin implementing today.

EMPOWERMENT PRAYER

Lord, I ask that You would make me a person of even greater conviction. That I would have enough self-worth and value for myself that I would stand by the boundaries I set, despite whatever obstacles may arise. Teach me to value the weight of my words and actions in setting these clear boundaries, and how they affect me and those I am in relationship with. Amen.

Day Twenty-Seven

HEED THE WARNING SIGNS

*Be sober, be vigilant; because your adversary
the devil walks about like a roaring lion,
seeking whom he may devour.*
—1 PETER 5:8

Discipline #27:
RECOGNIZE WHEN YOUR BOUNDARIES
ARE BEING CHALLENGED OR VIOLATED

Boundary lines can easily be violated or crossed if we are not
paying close attention. In First Peter 5:8, we discover that the
enemy cannot just infiltrate anyone's life; he is seeing whom he
may devour. This implies that we either grant him permission
or deny his access into our lives. Vigilance protects us from the
enemy's infiltration; it is something we must master if we are to
keep a close watch over our hearts and preserve the boundaries we have set for ourselves.

As we previously discussed, the key is to be unwavering and unwilling to compromise. There are those who will continually try to violate your lines of demarcation, who will push and test your limits, your patience, and your convictions. It may happen subtly over time or quite blatantly. Regardless of the circumstances, it is *your* job to keep watch; it is your responsibility to guard what you have fought to build. So again, be watchful, stay alert, and be aware! If you are not strong and firm in your boundaries, you will concede at the first sign of pressure. God's will is for you to be a person of fortitude and immovable conviction in every area of your life.

REFLECTION QUESTIONS

How do you handle stressful situations when people are pushing your boundaries?

_____

_____

_____

_____

_____

_____

_____

Are you steadfast enough in your own convictions to say "no" to someone you really care about?

_____

_____

Do you think that the paradigm of your own self-worth is in agreement with how God sees you?

How do you typically identify yourself in a family, group, or team setting?

ACTIVATION EXERCISES

Take a few moments to sit quietly before the Lord. Listen for His voice. Ask Him to show you your true identity and the ways in which you may have taken on a wrongful interpretation of who you really are. Write down what you feel He speaks to your heart.

EMPOWERMENT PRAYER

God, thank You for giving me a heart that loves truth. I ask that You would strengthen me and keep me watchful, alert, and aware of any attempts to cross my boundary lines. I want to be one who jealously guards my own heart; and in doing so, I would have the resiliency to create and abide by the boundaries needed to maintain health and wholeness in my life. Amen.

Day Twenty-Eight

LIVE ETHICALLY

For this is the love of God, that we keep His commandments. And His commandments are not burdensome.
—1 JOHN 5:3

Discipline #28:
LIVE ACCORDING TO GOD'S STANDARDS

God's ways are far above our own and are oftentimes hard to wrap our finite minds around. Even still, we trust that He is good in all things. His commandments are not a burden, purposed to restrain us. They are spiritual boundary lines of protection and preservation. God is for us, not against us. When our boundaries are in agreement with His, He empowers us to actually bring these things to pass. In our own lives, we some-times have to make decisions that cause pain and heartache, yet we are confident it is for our greater good; it *is* for the best.

Boundaries are there to keep you safe, to keep you protected. If you are not willing to make these difficult choices now, you are setting yourself up to be hurt in the days and years to come. To live according to God's standards means to live life on a higher plane. Part of living ethically is being a person of integrity. In other words, emotions, people, or situations do not control you; you dictate what you are controlled by. These boundaries help to maintain your self-respect and self-worth and keep you focused on the things that are most important.

REFLECTION QUESTIONS

Why is it important to "live ethically"?

_____

_____

_____

_____

_____

_____

What does this mean for you personally?

_____

_____

_____

_____

_____

_____

_____

How does this affect the daily decisions that you make?

_____

_____

_____

_____

_____

_____

_____

_____

In what way can making daily, godly choices change the trajectory of your life?

_____

_____

_____

_____

_____

_____

_____

_____

Activation Exercises

Take a moment and envision yourself ten years from now. What does your life look like? Have your decisions bettered your life or have they taken you down a negative path? Have you met your goals? Would you be happy moving forward in the same way you are right now? It's important to realize that your daily decisions have long-lasting repercussions. God is there to help and guide you, but ultimately you are responsible for the choices that steer the course of your life.

Empowerment Prayer

Lord, I ask that You would help me to make decisions that will bear lasting fruit. That I would not simply move on emotion, but I would be led by Your Spirit. Help me to make godly choices that are governed by wisdom and that will steer me on the right course. Thank You for Your faithfulness and for never giving up on me. You are good, always. Amen.

Day Twenty-Nine

CLEARLY SET YOUR LIMITS

Blessed is the man who walks not in the counsel of the ungodly, nor stands in the path of sinners, nor sits in the seat of the scornful; but his delight is in the law of the Lord, and in His law he meditates day and night.
—PSALMS 1:1-2

Discipline #29:
PLAY TO AN AUDIENCE OF ONE—THE ONE

In our relationships, we often feel pulled in multiple directions—or that we *owe* others our undivided focus and attention. This is the genesis of dysfunctional relationships. We are first and foremost in relationship with God. If there is anything we *owe*, it is our allegiance to Him. Our time, attention, emotions, and energy should never be poured out on people more than they are on Him. When He is our priority, boundaries will come into focus. God's centrality and supremacy in our lives serves as the foundation out of which all boundaries emerge. It is where our priorities are birthed.

A large part of this Christian walk is firmly grasping what our priorities should be, and how to practically apply them on a daily basis (see Matt. 4:10; 6:33). The people in our lives are significant and important, but if they are taking the place that rightfully belongs to God, or putting you in a place only God should occupy, you are setting yourself up for relational disaster. Keep God in His rightful place, and everything else will fall into its proper place.

REFLECTION QUESTIONS

How do you prioritize your relationships?

_____

_____

_____

_____

_____

_____

In what ways do your relational priorities affect your spiritual life?

_____

_____

_____

_____

_____

Why is it important to make God your first priority?

How do you think this changes the way you function as a Christian?

Activation Exercises

Make a list (and be honest) of your relational priorities, and start with the most important to you. For example, who is the first person you think of when you wake up in the morning?

Now, take that same list and re-order it if you think it needs some re-ordering. How will you begin to make these changes in your life?

Empowerment Prayer

Father, help me to keep You at the center of my life, and give me a heart that seeks You first. Above anyone and above anything—I want You to have the first place in my heart, the place that is rightfully Yours. Help me to prioritize my life according to Your kingdom, that I would be one who learns how to love well. I want to be a true friend of God who displays Your heart rightly to those around me. Amen.

RESPECT OTHERS' BOUNDARIES

Love others as well as you love yourself.
—Matthew 22:39, MSG

Discipline #30:
HONOR THE BOUNDARIES OF OTHERS

Loving each other can appear simple enough at first glance. It comes easier for some than others. But in actuality, the ability to love others begins with the ability to first love *yourself*…which for some is a major hurdle to scale. We all have stories to tell that are marked by joy, pain, triumph, and tragedy. Our experiences play a large part in shaping who we become, and these experiences also shape how we see ourselves. For many of us, deep down there is an inability to love ourselves at a heart level—and this has a profound effect on our outward relationships.

The first step in learning how to honor and respect someone else and their boundaries is discovering your own self-worth. If you do not believe that you are worthy of protective boundaries that deserved to be honored, you will not respect the boundaries of other people. The dynamic of honoring someone else's boundary lines will never be reproduced in your relationships until you are able to see yourself worthy of that same respect and honor.

REFLECTION QUESTIONS

When you think of yourself—physical characteristics, personality, character qualities, etc.—what comes to mind? Are they positive thoughts or negative thoughts?

_____

_____

_____

_____

_____

_____

_____

At the very root, do you feel like you can truly say that you love yourself and consider your boundaries worth respecting? Why or why not?

_____

_____

_____

_____

_____

_____

_____

_____

_____

What hinders you from actually loving yourself?

_____

_____

_____

_____

_____

_____

_____

_____

_____

_____

_____

_____

_____

Activation Exercises

If God were to look at you right now, in this moment, what would He see? Don't answer this question from your perspective, but from His. How do you think God really sees you? Ask Him to reveal who you really are. Write down what comes to mind at this very moment. Do not edit. Do you see a difference between your perception and God's perspective? What is that difference?

Empowerment Prayer

God, I ask that You would give me a deeper revelation of Your love for me, that You would begin to transform the way I see myself. Show me how to see me through Your eyes, that I might see myself worthy of love, respect, and honor. Break off the lies and mindsets that keep me from feeling accepted. Teach me how to honor myself, that in turn I might honor others with that same measure of radical love. I want to be someone who loves extravagantly, unhindered by past pain and hurt. Thank You that Your perfect love casts out all fear, and that in You I find true worth and acceptance. Amen.

Day Thirty-One

KEEP A POSITIVE EXPECTATION

Now faith is the substance of things hoped for....
—HEBREWS 11:1

Discipline #31:
LET HOPE INTRODUCE YOU TO
A NEW WAY OF LIVING

"What happens to a dream deferred? Does it dry up like a raisin in the sun? Or fester like a sore—and then run? Does it stink like rotten meat? Or crust and sugar over—like a syrupy sweet? Maybe it just sags like a heavy load. Or does it explode?" —LANGSTON HUGHES

Living from a place of hope is the fruit of a life that is grounded in Christ. Why? Because He is hope personified. He is the hope that *never* disappoints! When we place our hopes and expectations in mere human beings, we will almost always be disappointed—because human beings are imperfect and we all make mistakes. To live in true freedom, our hope must always be found in Christ alone. Many relational soul ties begin because we believe the lie that a person is worthy of our unwavering hope and confidence. This is not true, for a person can never deliver on such high expectations—only God can.

Hopelessness is a byproduct of disillusionment. When you experience disappointment over and over again, your heart becomes bitter and calloused, and you lose sight of the true nature of God. Living from a place of hope means letting go of past disappointments and choosing to start fresh. It means allowing yourself to dream, to believe, and to expect extraordinary things. Expand your vision and allow yourself to believe for God's best! He does not bring His people out of bondage only to bring them into a place of hopelessness. His will is for you to live in a place of hope, where He is the anchor of your soul (see Heb. 6:19).

REFLECTION QUESTIONS

Do you expect to be disappointed or hurt in your relationships? Why do you feel this way?

_____

_____

_____

_____

_____

_____

_____

Do you have dreams that you've let go of?

_____

_____

_____

_____

_____

What in your past (or present) has caused you to approach life this way?

_____

_____

_____

_____

What dreams have you deferred and why?

_____

_____

_____

_____

_____

_____

_____

Activation Exercises

Ask the Holy Spirit to reveal to you the root of disappointment or hopelessness in your life. Where/when did it begin for you? Let Him walk you through the pain of those difficult moments and circumstances, and bring healing to those wounds. It is something that cripples our ability to be successful or to be truly happy, so it is vital that we deal with these issues in our hearts. *God wants you to hope again.*

Empowerment Prayer

Father, I ask that You would expose the roots of hopelessness and disappointment in my life. Take away the pain of past hurts that have caused me not to trust You. Wash away the brokenness of shattered dreams and deferred hopes. Thank You, God, that You promise beauty for ashes. I ask now that You would take my heart and immerse me in Your steadfast love. Show me how to trust in Your goodness once again. Let fresh rivers of hope be released in my heart. Amen.

Day Thirty-Two

SEE PAST BARRIERS

Assuredly, I say to you, if you have faith as a
mustard seed, you will say to this mountain,
"Move from here to there," and it will move;
and nothing will be impossible for you.
—MATTHEW 17:20

Discipline #32:
BREAK THROUGH BOUNDARIES
BY FOLLOWING THE SPIRIT

Faith has the ability to take us beyond what we can see with our natural eyes. It gives us the power and permission to believe for things we never thought possible. That is the essence of faith. It believes that *all* things are possible. Sometimes we are blinded by fears, by intimidation, by circumstance, and in turn we cannot see past the barriers before us. They tower over us like mountains that appear immovable. But we know with God there is no such thing as impossibility. He is God. He is not moved by impossibilities. Impossibilities are moved by Him! (See Matthew 19:26.)

Often, it takes a leap of faith to see beyond the natural and believe for the supernatural. The Spirit of God is released by and works according to our faith; the moment we believe, in that instant, we can break down barriers that have held us captive for years. All it takes is getting beyond the barrier of our belief systems or past the prisons of our paradigms. It takes breaking down the walls of our finite imaginations and letting our hearts be led by the Spirit of God to see with new eyes— eyes of faith.

REFLECTION QUESTIONS

Do you often struggle to have faith for things?

_____

_____

_____

_____

In what area has your faith shriveled up like a raisin in the sun?

_____

_____

_____

_____

_____

Does the word "impossibility" have a negative connotation for you? If yes, why?

_____

_____

_____

_____

What do you think causes you to struggle with walking in faith?

_____

_____

_____

_____

_____

What are the barriers in your life that keep you from moving in faith?

_____

_____

_____

_____

_____

_____

_____

Activation Exercises

As an exercise in faith, think of something that seems impossible in the natural that you would like to see happen. Write it down. Set a reminder and commit to pray consistently for this particular need over the next twenty-one days. Faith is something that needs to be exercised like a muscle, and prayer is one of the most powerful tools to accomplish this.

Reflection Prayer

Lord, I ask You to give me eyes of faith to see like You do. I need Your help to see beyond my own understanding and limited way of thinking. You see far beyond what my eyes can see; please, Lord, remove whatever is standing in the way of me walking in the Spirit and experiencing the breakthrough that is available to me. Help me to step beyond what is comfortable, as I trust You to lead me. Amen.

Day Thirty-Three

FOLLOW GOD'S LEAD

God's Spirit beckons. There are things
to do and places to go!
—Romans 8:14, MSG

Discipline #33:
TRANSFER COMPLETE CONTROL
TO THE HOLY SPIRIT

When we choose to walk in the Spirit, we essentially give up our need to maintain control of our lives. This is not an invitation to a disorderly, chaotic life; it is the opposite. We are actually stepping into a higher order—the order of God. Transferring control of our lives over to God gives the Holy Spirit free access to move in our life in supernatural ways; we become vessels and conduits for Him to work through. When we claim that we want to let the Spirit move but we give Him limited access, we actually put up barriers and restraints instead of granting Him freedom. It's like unlocking a door, but keeping it shut with an "Enter at your own risk" or "Do not disturb" sign posted on the outside. It conveys, "I want you here, but only on my terms."

Perhaps in the past other people or addictions or bondages have controlled you. Maybe your life was governed by different perspectives, paradigms, or mindsets. As you have received freedom from those restraining agents, it is time for you to make a choice—will you live in freedom, as one yielded to the Holy Spirit, or will you position yourself to re-enter the cycle?

Living a life that is led by the Spirit opens our eyes to new dimensions. It allows us to live from heaven to earth instead of from earth to heaven. A life surrendered to the Holy Spirit is how we live in heavenly places, seated with Christ. In this way, we are not inhibited by this world, but release heaven as the Spirit works through us. This was the example that Jesus modeled for us, and it is how we were meant to operate in our everyday Christian lives.

REFLECTION QUESTIONS

What hinders you from giving up full control to the Holy Spirit?

_____

_____

_____

_____

_____

_____

_____

What are you holding onto that could preempt His presence? (Relationships? Mindsets? Unforgiveness?)

_____

_____

_____

_____

_____

What are you afraid will happen if you let go of your emotions, ego, or etiquette?

_____

_____

_____

_____

In what ways have you previously quenched or restrained the Spirit from having full access in your life? (See 1 Thessalonians 5:19.)

_____

_____

_____

_____

_____

ACTIVATION EXERCISES

Practice listening to the voice of the Holy Spirit. Ask Him a specific question. It can be something simple such as, "Holy Spirit, what do You want to say/do through me today?" In order to walk with Him, it is crucial that we learn to recognize the way He speaks to us. This may look different for everyone. It may be a whisper, it may be a picture in your mind, it may be a scripture, etc. Start writing down what the Holy Spirit says to you and *how* He speaks.

EMPOWERMENT PRAYER

Holy Spirit, open my eyes that I might see with clarity. I want to work with You and move with You where You lead me. Help me to give You full control and access into every area of my life, nothing withheld. I want to walk in the fullness of Your Spirit, that I would be able to release the kingdom of God to those around me, wherever I go. Teach me to hear Your voice and to listen when You speak. Help me not to quench Your Spirit. Amen.

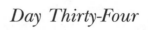

Day Thirty-Four

LEAN IN

Embrace this God-life. Really embrace it,
and nothing will be too much for you.
—MARK 11:22, MSG

Discipline #34:
BEGIN TO LIVE LIFE GOD'S WAY

The key to living life "God's way" is through intimacy with Him. When we connect deeply with a person, we begin to know their thoughts, their desires, their plans, and their dreams. Why should it be any different with God? In the same way we might have shared our lives with other people who created harmful, bondage-creating soul ties, the greatest exchange of intimacy is reserved for you and your Maker. When we are immersed in God's presence, it drives out all fear, all anxiety, all confusion, and all of the hindrances that keep us from walking out a life-style that is fully focused on Jesus. When we learn to live from a place that leans on Him, it makes room for us to live outside of our own paradigms.

Our dependency produces a yielding to the ways of God, which in turn produces intimacy that is built on trust. But intimacy with God, as we know from any relationship, has to be cultivated, watered, and fed. He wants us to engage in a lifestyle that reflects who He is and what He's done for us, on a daily basis. The encounters with God we experience are not meant to satisfy simply a momentary need or longing. They are meant to be carried with us throughout our entire lives. This empowers us to walk in a sustained place of freedom that we could not access before.

REFLECTION QUESTIONS

What does "intimacy with God" look like for you?

_____

_____

_____

_____

_____

What are you doing to cultivate this lifestyle of intimacy with God?

_____

_____

_____

_____

_____

_____

_____

_____

Do you find it difficult to be dependent on God? If you answered "yes," why?

_____

_____

_____

_____

_____

How can you learn to live by pursuing intimacy with God?

_____

_____

_____

_____

_____

_____

_____

Activation Exercises

Ask the Holy Spirit to show you your need for God; let Him strip away the stumbling block of self-sufficiency. Our dependency on God comes from the knowledge that we cannot do it on our own apart from Him. The act of "leaning in" to Him is the ultimate form of surrender and act of humility. But it comes from a place of total trust in the One we are leaning on.

Reflection Prayer

Lord, thank You for Your faithfulness and that You will never leave me. Break down the barriers that stand in the way of me completely leaning into and onto You. I place my complete dependency upon You, and ask that You would show me how to walk in Your ways. Help me to live a life that reflects Your glory and Your nature to the world around me. Amen.

Day Thirty-Five

STEP OUT

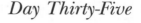

*God's Spirit is on me; he's chosen me to preach
the Message of good news to the poor, sent me to
announce pardon to prisoners and recovery of
sight to the blind, to set the burdened and battered
free, to announce, "This is God's year to act!"*
—LUKE 4:18, MSG

Discipline #35:
ACTIVATE THE POWER OF GOD WITHIN YOU

God desires that we would live a life of abundance, full of promise, full of hope, and full of power. Hope itself, with the right expression, is an unbreakable force. It is a gift that can see the blessing of God in the darkest of circumstances because it carries with it the vision of a God who is greater than any storm we face. It is this same hope that should cause us to seek the hurting and to see the broken made whole.

When we have a grasp on exactly what it is that we carry within us—the weight and glory of heaven itself—it ignites a passion within us to see this abundance overflow to those in our sphere of influence. It is not something meant to be contained within the four walls of our physical church buildings or synagogues; the power of God is meant to be experienced by all people—*on earth as it is in heaven.* This was the mandate given to Jesus; the same mandate He gave His twelve disciples—and this same mandate still rings true for us today.

What's the key to releasing His power in your life? Step out. Believe He's with you. Trust that the Holy Spirit lives within you. The power of God that broke every chain and soul entanglement *for* you wants to release this same chain-breaking power *through* you.

REFLECTION QUESTIONS

What does hope look like for you?

_____

_____

_____

_____

_____

How does hope change your mindset about how you live or what's important?

_____

_____

_____

How does hope change your perspective of the future?

What do you think it looks like to walk in the power of God?

How can you bring hope to others on a daily basis?

Activation Exercises

What was it that Jesus carried that allowed Him to operate in such divine alignment with heaven? *The Holy Spirit.* You have this same ability living inside of you (see 1 John 4:4). And again, it starts with understanding the power that is available to you. It starts with being a willing vessel. Ask yourself, "What have I received from the power of God?" Hopefully, by this point in the journey, you have experienced a measure of freedom and deliverance from whatever was holding your soul hostage. Your freedom and your breakthrough are to be enjoyed—and they are to be stewarded. Write down what God is doing in your life right now. Be specific. Why? Because He wants to use you to set others free from the same things. Your testimony is what you offer to those who are in the same place of bondage that you were.

Empowerment Prayer

Lord, thank You that You've made heaven available to me right here and now. I ask that You would show me how to release Your presence and Your kingdom to those around me. I want to walk in power like You did. I want to be a carrier of hope to those who have lost it. Show me how to use my testimony, my story, my deliverance, and my breakthrough as a tool to bring hope to the hopeless and freedom to the captive, that they would find new life and trust, once again, in You. Amen.

Day Thirty-Six

LISTEN

And behold, the Lord passed by, and a great and strong wind tore into the mountains and broke the rocks in pieces before the Lord, but the Lord was not in the wind; and after the wind an earthquake, but the Lord was not in the earthquake; and after the earthquake a fire, but the Lord was not in the fire; and after the fire a still small voice.

—1 KINGS 19:11-12

Discipline #36:
HONESTLY EVALUATE YOUR
SOUL'S CONDITION

The soul is essentially the barometer for our lives; it steers the course of our minds, hearts, wills, and emotions. Throughout the course of daily life, we have a tendency to hit "auto-pilot" and ignore the reality of what is happening within the recesses of our soul. It's not something that most of us attend to on a regular basis. But in actuality, it affects us much more than we know. In order to live from a place of true freedom and authenticity, we have to keep watch over our own souls. We have to be aware of their true condition. When this is ignored, we easily hold on to strongholds that God wants to set us free from.

To reclaim your soul demands interior honesty. Everything you have learned so far about different soul ties, the need for boundaries, and pressing into God must be honestly evaluated. Take an internal inventory and see what strongholds or ties are still present. Ask the Holy Spirit to reveal what remains to be healed. We will never walk in freedom if we cannot acknowledge the true condition of our bondage. Admittance is 80 percent of our deliverance. God wants to remove every agent and avenue of bondage and replace it with His life, His kingdom, His power, His gifts, His fruit, His freedom, and His wholeness. Deliverance is an invitation to receive an extraordinary divine exchange.

REFLECTION QUESTIONS

If you were to evaluate the condition of your soul right now, how would you describe it?

_____

_____

_____

_____

_____

_____

_____

_____

Do you have an appetite for spiritual things?

_____

_____

_____

_____

_____

Do you feel you can easily connect with the Holy Spirit?

_____

_____

_____

_____

_____

What is the first word or thought that comes to mind when you think of prayer? These are some telling signs of the state and condition of your heart!

_____

_____

_____

_____

_____

What are you prepared to give up in exchange for the wonderful gifts and fruit God has in store for you?

_____

_____

_____

_____

_____

ACTIVATION EXERCISES

Take a good thirty minutes (or whatever time you can allot) and sit quietly before the Lord. Search your heart and intentionally evaluate the condition of your soul. Do you hunger for God? Do you enjoy the spiritual disciplines of reading His Word and prayer? Do you pursue His presence? Or are these things more like a chore or duty? Take some time to journal your thoughts. What is God speaking to you?

EMPOWERMENT PRAYER

Lord, I ask that You make me a person who jealously guards the condition of my soul. I want to be awake and alert. I want to have a passion for You that cannot be quenched by anything else. Help me to keep watch over my soul, that I would not allow anything to turn my attention away from the deeper things of You. Give me an undivided focus to pursue You with all of my mind, heart, will, and strength. You are worthy of all my affections. I love you wholeheartedly. Amen.

Day Thirty-Seven

FORGIVE

*Remember, the Lord forgave you, so
you must forgive others.*
—Colossians 3:13, NLT

Discipline #37:
EXERCISE YOUR AUTHORITY TO FORGIVE

Forgiveness is absolutely essential in the process of moving toward wholeness and freedom. When you hold on to unforgiveness, it's like setting up an impassible roadblock in the middle of a busy street. It stops the flow of traffic, not only for you, but for those on the other side as well.

There are myriad reasons why a person chooses not to forgive. Pain is real, and hurts can go very deep. But what many fail to realize is that the choice to hold on to unforgiveness, bitterness, and resentment cripples them from moving forward entirely. We all want to step into the plan of God for our future, but we must first exercise our authority to break agreement with the past through forgiveness.

Exercising the power to forgive can break the chains of years of bondage. While it can be one of the most difficult things to do, it is also one of the most important. In fact, there is a grace for forgiveness. Just as there is a grace, or supernatural empowerment, for you to model the character of Christ in other areas, there is a divine empowerment available to you the moment you exercise the choice to forgive.

REFLECTION QUESTIONS

Are there individuals whom you have not forgiven?

_____

_____

_____

_____

_____

Why have you been unwilling or unable to forgive?

_____

_____

_____

_____

_____

_____

How has this affected your spiritual walk?

Do think this has affected the other person(s) as well? How so?

How can forgiving someone set you free from being held captive to the past?

Activation Exercises

Forgiveness is about release. Every time a situation crosses your mind that causes the pain of yesterday to flood your soul today (overwhelming your thoughts and emotions with hurt, bitterness, anger, and resentment) say out loud, "I release _____ (call their name) for _____" (be specific about what they said and did). Do it every time you think those thoughts or feel those emotions (see Matt. 18:22). You will find that days, weeks, and even months will have gone by and those thoughts and emotions are no longer pervading your life.

Empowerment Prayer

God, I ask for the grace to forgive those who have hurt me. I don't want to hold on to bitterness and anger any longer. I want to walk in freedom. I exercise the authority to forgive. I thank You that supernatural empowerment is available the moment I choose to make this God-honoring decision. I release those who have caused me pain, and I let go of the past I've held on to so tightly. Today I am choosing to forgive. I am choosing to walk in love.

Jesus, Your blood paid my debt and still covers a multitude of sins today; so I plead Your blood over my heart and over every person who has wronged me, past and present. Thank You for Your saving grace, and thank You for making it possible for me to walk in forgiveness, just as You forgave me. Amen.

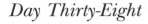

Day Thirty-Eight

ABIDE

*May God himself, the God who makes everything
holy and whole, make you holy and whole, put you
together—spirit, soul, and body—and keep you
fit for the coming of our Master, Jesus Christ.*
—1 THESSALONIANS 5:23, MSG

Discipline #38:
KNOW GOD'S WILL BY REMAINING
IN GOD'S WORD

Abiding in Christ is the foundation of our relationship with
Him (see John 15:7-10; Ps. 91:1). It's the key that unlocks His
heart! When we learn the art of abiding in Him, we know His
voice, we know His heart, we know His ways, and we know
His will. His Word contains the truth we need for every circumstance, every trial, and every cry of our heart. When we

understand this reality, we begin to pray from a place of knowledge and spiritual confidence.

Prayer is what moves the heart of God to act on behalf of His children; it's the language of heaven. When we know His heart, we are able to pray with boldness because we know He hears and will answer such prayers. God will surely answer God. In other words, when we pray in agreement and alignment with things God would pray Himself (were He praying), we can be sure that He *will* answer. He *will* accomplish what He *wills*.

God is looking for people to pray for His will to be done— who would know Him so deeply that His will actually becomes their will. We discover this, most clearly, by spending time in His Word. This is truly abiding in God, for as we spend time in His Word, His Word starts to spend time *in us*. In this lifetime we can only but scratch the surface of all God is. But it is truly our great privilege to search Him out and to seek Him. And in seeking, we have the promise that we will find Him.

REFLECTION QUESTIONS

How do you approach Bible study? Is it stale, dry, and boring—or is it a fountain and source of life for you?

_____

_____

_____

_____

_____

_____

_____

_____

_____

_____

_____

_____

When you pray, is it from a place of confidence, or do you find yourself constantly adding, "If it be Thy will" to a prayer? (One would only pray this if they did not know His will. While there are some areas of mystery concerning God's will, there are many aspects of His will revealed in His Word.)

_____

_____

_____

_____

_____

_____

_____

_____

_____

_____

Activation Exercises

Open your Bible to a passage of scripture that has significance to you. Read through the passage and let the Holy Spirit speak fresh revelation to you. Even if you have read the verse thousands of times, enter into this time with fresh expectation that He will speak and that your time in God's Word is a divine setup to practice the art of *abiding in God*. Begin to dialogue with God about the passage and how it relates to your walk with Him and your life.

Empowerment Prayer

Lord, thank You for the incredible gift of being able to know You, that in all Your greatness Your deep desire is the affection of the human heart. I want to know and experience Your ways, not just read about them in the pages of the Bible. Teach me how to truly abide in You and in Your Word. Open the Bible up to me in a way I have never experienced before, that I might pray with confidence and learn what moves Your heart...and how to boldly pray Your will on the earth. Amen.

Day Thirty-Nine

BIND

And I will give you the keys of the kingdom of heaven,
and whatever you bind on earth will be bound in heaven,
and whatever you loose on earth will be loosed in heaven.
—MATTHEW 16:19

Discipline # 39:
IDENTIFY ENEMIES OF YOUR SOUL
THAT NEED TO BE BOUND

In order to defeat the strongholds in your soul, you must first be able to identify them. It is vital you know what specific things are holding you captive in order to break free from them. The enemy seeks to keep these things hidden and to keep you in darkness so that you cannot bring these strongholds into the light and experience victory. As long as you remain blind, you are unable to bind. Once you know what you are up against, you can take the necessary steps to bind them by name and break free from what has held you captive.

The enemy understands the authority you possess to derail every strategy of darkness. Satan himself holds no authority or power; he only has what you give him access to—whether consciously or not. It is imperative that you know how to wage war on the enemy of your soul. He is relentless, and is out to destroy you in every way possible. But he never has the final word because the blood of Jesus secured his fate and our redemption all in one. Your victory has already been bought and paid for!

REFLECTION QUESTIONS

When we talk about the "strong man" and things that keep our souls bound, what specifically comes to mind?

_____

_____

_____

_____

_____

Can you identify these types of bondages in your soul? If so, write these down. This is a starting place for the binding process. As long as you can identify them, you can bind them.

_____

_____

_____

_____

_____

_____

_____

_____

_____

_____

_____

_____

_____

_____

_____

_____

_____

_____

_____

ACTIVATION EXERCISES

A large part of being able to bind strongholds comes from understanding your identity. It is important that you recognize who you are in Christ and exercise the authority that's rightfully been given to you. Ask the Lord to give you a greater understanding of this authority, who you are in Him, and the true power you have to conquer the enemies of your soul. Now, it's time to step out and bind these enemies.

In Jesus' Name, I identify and bind:

_____

_____

_____

_____

_____

_____

_____

_____

_____

_____

_____

EMPOWERMENT PRAYER

Thank You, Lord, for the price You paid for my freedom. Bondage is not Your will. Oppression is not Your will. A captive soul is not Your will. Because of the price You paid on the cross, I have the authority to defeat anything that threatens to oppress me or hold me captive. I ask that You would give me an even greater understanding of my identity in You, that I would never again be bound by any type of enslaving spirit or entanglement, but instead would walk in freedom, deliverance, and liberty. Amen.

Day Forty

PRAY

The earnest prayer of a righteous person has great power and produces wonderful results.
—James 5:16, NLT

Discipline #40:
RECLAIM YOUR SOUL USING THE WEAPON OF PRAYER

Prayer is a powerful weapon, and one that moves the heart of God like no other. When we pray, angels and demons move at the sound of our voices. The spirit realm shifts, and as a result the natural world is impacted. Our prayers carry and release a power that we can barely glimpse now. We know that prayer is the catalyst that brings the resources of heaven into the earth. One of the places this begins is in your soul. Now that you have bound every soul tie, every form of bondage, every destructive form of captivity, it is time for you to loose the peace and power of heaven.

In heaven there is perfect peace. There is soundness. There is order. Chaos is absent. Torment and bondage are non-existent. If these realities are non-existent in the place of heaven, they should likewise be non-existent in one who houses the glorious down payment of heaven—the Holy Spirit. It is time for you to enjoy every benefit and blessing of heaven *on earth*, starting in the place of your soul. You have bound the strong man; now, it's time to release the Spirit. The key is coming into agreement with everything He offers.

Scripture reveals that you are the temple of the Holy Spirit. We know that He is the One who makes it possible for your spirit to be saved. That said, He is also responsible for transforming *every* area of your life, body, soul and spirit, bringing His order and kingdom to these three realms. My desire is that, through prayer, you would loose the power, the peace, and the freedom of heaven into your soul. It's available. I invite you to receive it, release it, and experience the lifestyle of freedom that God has willed for you!

REFLECTION QUESTIONS

How does prayer impact your soul? (Once bondages and soul ties are bound, what role does prayer place in *loosing* God's kingdom?)

_____

_____

_____

_____

_____

_____

What would it look like for you to experience heaven in your soul? Take a few minutes to seriously think about this, and then write down what you've envisioned.

ACTIVATION EXERCISES

Reflect for a moment on the power of prayer. If you haven't already, set aside a block of time each day to spend in prayer—dedicating a certain amount of your time with God to loosing what's in heaven *into* your soul. In the same way that we have gone through an extensive 40-day process to experience freedom in your soul, you must steward this freedom by proactively releasing the kingdom of God, and all of its resources, into your soul. Peace. Joy. Freedom. Rest. Order. Ask the Holy Spirit for insight into what or how to pray for *your* soul and declare these things over yourself.

EMPOWERMENT PRAYER

Lord, thank You for giving me the ability to release the resources of heaven into my soul through prayer. Holy Spirit, You live inside of me. You are with me. You are transforming me spirit, soul, and body. In this season, I focus on my soul being conformed into the image of Christ. Thank You for giving me a visual of what You desire to release into my soul—Your kingdom of righteousness, peace, and joy in the Holy Spirit (see Rom. 14:17). So I pray, Your kingdom come, Your will be done, on earth, and in my soul, as it is in heaven. Amen.

ABOUT THE AUTHOR

As a best-selling author, keynote speaker, and former senator of Bermuda, Dr. Trimm is a sought-after empowerment specialist, thought leader, and advocate for cultural change. Listed among *Ebony* magazine's Power 100 as the "top 100 doers and influencers in the world today," Dr. Trimm consults with civic, nonprofit, and religious leaders around the world. With a background in government, education, psychology, and human development, Dr. Trimm translates powerful spiritual truth into everyday language that empowers individuals to transform their lives and their communities.

Trimm International is a pioneering force in the personal and leadership development field. On the forefront of transforming culture through empowering individuals to lead change, Trimm International provides cutting-edge programs and innovative products that inspire, equip, and empower people to impact their world.